John

UNTIL WE LEARN
TO RISE

Short Poems on Life and Love

Michael J. Farrand

Cosmic Burst Press

Enjoy!!

Michael J. Farrand

To my Muse.

"Who loves, raves."

GEORGE GORDON "LORD BYRON" (1788 – 1824)

CONTENTS

PREFACE

Three poems have been removed for this edition and remaining poems proofed for word choice and formatting. Other changes to the manuscript have resulted from application of different software and updates in the various platforms used.

I LOVE YOU

I love you
and always have,
from the moment
our eyes met.

And everything
since that day
has been about you:
The things I do
The words I say
My every thought
from day-to-day.

BACKWARDS

.backwards everything doing always i'M

Figure 1 – Cart Before Horse

BOOM, POP, KAPOW!

Boom, pop, kapow!
　Oh, man, wow
　　Look what you did.

Figure 2- Jour de l'an feux d'artifice, Québec

THE LOWLY FRUIT FLY

The lowly fruit fly goes
Through the things through which we go
(But with a touch less ego.)

Figure 3 - Ceratitis capitata

MAY GOD STRIKE
ME DEAD

If I should ever . .
  Fail to be grateful
    Become mean and hateful
      Overlook the fateful.

If I should ever . .
  Go off my head
    Cause pain instead
      May God strike me dead.

© 2001

Figure 4 - Lightning storm over Boston

MY FAVORITE PASTIME

All of my friends
Are whitewater rafting
For a very special fare
   Free! they said
   But not for me
For I would not take the dare.

Better to sit
And think about you
My favorite pastime
   Without that
   My life would be through
And wouldn't be worth a dime.

© 2001

Figure 5 - White Water Rafting, Kamimoku, Gunma, Japan

TRAPEZE

My trapeze I lower
  Into your circus
    The net I promise to place there
    And if you should grab
  My outstretched hand
Your life will be mine to share.

© 2001

Figure 6 - Rony Roller Circus

A COUNTRY LANE

We could walk
a country lane
We could talk
amidst the rain
We could balk
and pitch the pain
We could stalk
the truth again.

Figure 7 - Country Lane Kentucky

NOW THAT I'VE BEHELD YOU

He had a lot of practice,
God did
Creating wonderful things
Cashews, the lemon, honey, Elvis,
the violin.

Each one of these was practice,
I see
Now that I've beheld you
Each one of these preliminary
to His real challenge
Which was you.

AN ACTRESS FROM MANHATTAN

There once was an actress from Manhattan
My wallet she intentionally flattened
   Her career went nowhere
   So she restyled her hair
Now she storms the divorce courts like Patton.

© 2002

Figure 8 – Times Square NYC 1977

THE WRONG STAR

I'm thinking
   You hitched your wagon
      To the wrong star.

And when
  You hitch your wagon
      To the wrong star,

Your wheels bog down
  In waist-deep mud
      And you don't get very far.

© 2002

YOUR COTTON GIN

Yes, of course
I'm volunteering
When I should
Instead be fearing
Knowing well
The pain I'll be in
When you catch me
Disappearing
Into your cotton gin.

© 2002

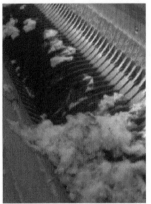

Figure 9 - Burton Cotton Gin

DO YOU REALLY THINK IT'S TOO LATE?

You said it your way
   I said it mine
      Neither wanting to put it straight.

So you went your way
   And I went mine
      Do you really think it's too late?

© 2003

FROM HERE TO KANKAKEE

If I could write a poem that would make the World feel
What it's like to be hugged by you
I would get no more hugs
That much is clear
For the line would stretch from here to Kankakee.

© 2003

Figure 10 - Марш мира Москва 21 сент 2014

IF LOVE WERE A
LOGICAL PROCESS

If love were a
   Logical process
There would be no
   Broken hearts

But, if love were a
   Logical process
There would be no
   Hearts to break(!)

© 2003

LOVE HOOKS

Little looks
Corner nooks
Rippling brooks
Trembling schnooks
Raging chinooks
Soft nainsooks
French cooks
Poetry books
Love hooks.

© 2003

Figure 11 - Dining Nook

MAINTAINING
POSITION

We don't exist!
  Exclaimed the phenomenon
    to the legend.

After me I insist!
  Proclaimed the legend,
    maintaining position.

© 2003

MY RESTING QUILL

I thought, perhaps
The day would come
My pen, the ink would dry
Thoughts that flowed
Like buttered rum
Would cease their asking *why*.

But, just when
My head goes hush
My pen sits quietly still
Just then, the words they gush
And power my resting quill.

© 2003

Figure 12 - Untitled (cropped)

REGRETS

Regrets
   That's where I spend my days
      Regretting what I've done
         Regretting what I've said.

         I use regrets
      To punish me, myself
   For being way too slow
(For being scared to grow.)

© 2003

GOTTA FIND
SOMETHIN' TO DO

Gotta find somethin' to do
In between
Thinkin' about you
and
Thinkin' about you.

Gotta find somethin' to do
Or maybe I'll just . .

Think about you.

EEK AND SUPER EEK

Eek and Super Eek
   Went out for a midnight stroll
You know, Eek said Super Eek
   Our life, it is so droll.

You scare people a little bit
   Then I fire grapeshot
      Pretty soon hysteria's
         The sum of what we've got!

© 2006

Figure 13 - SCREAM!

HOW MUCH LIVING
HAVE YOU SEEN

How much living have you seen
  Are you blue
    Or are you green?

© 2006

A PICTURE OF YOU

Today I saw a picture of you
  Three, in fact
    Together.

Your eyes, your soul, your sun
  Cut through
    My heart
      In stormy weather.

© 2006

Figure 14 - Robert Cornelius (1809–1893)

AS GOOD A POET BE

If I could as good a poet be
  As the Muse you've been to me.

© 2007

BLACK CLOUD

Black cloud,
  Black cloud
    Why so blue?

© 2007

Figure 15 - Very Black Clouds Looming

ENDING BY DUMAS?

Beginnings by Dickens.
Middle Kafkaesque.
Ending by Dumas?

Figure 16 - Chocolate Coins

I KNOW WHAT IT WAS

I know what it *was*
   I heard the *hum*
     I felt the *buzz.*

And just because
   I know what *was*
     I keep the flame
Just because.

© 2007

WOULD YOU HAVE ME

Would you have me without warts
  All the longs without the shorts
    All the ups without the downs
      All the cities without the towns?

Would you have me perfection-based
  All my silliness erased
    Or would you take me as I am
      A flawed, unpolished gem?

© 2007

Figure 17 - 4E2A7069s (cropped)

ELVIS FLIPPING BURGERS

I saw Elvis flipping burgers
  At the Corner burger store
I saw Edgar sipping absinthe
  While a crow shrieked *Nevermore!*
I saw Thomas strum a fiddle
  Behind Sally Hemings' door
    Gee, I must be dreaming
    We're not in Kansas anymore.

© 2008

Figure 18 - Blue Moon Diner

PARENTS IN RETREAT

Kids on drugs
   Kids in jail
      Kids out in the street
      Minus hugs
   Minus bail
Parents in retreat.

© 2014

Figure 19 - Uteliggeren

BAD FOR MY ESTATE

If I'm outside
   I'm spending
      At a very rapid rate
Good for those vending
(Bad for my estate.)

© 2014

Figure 20 - Louis Marx House

IT GOES ON

He said a great thing about Life
. Robert Frost, the poet, I mean
.. he said that through discord
... pain and
.... strife
... no matter the trouble you've seen
.. only one thing he'd learned
. about Life, that is:
It goes on.

© 2014

Figure 21 - Robert Frost

THE KIND OF LOOKS

The kind of looks that slay a man
   That make him spend the rent
The kind that make him say *Amen!*
   That money was well spent.

© 2014

Figure 22 - beautiful faces

GROW SOME GUTS

Having made the turn on *Crazy*
And closed the book on *Nuts*
Goodbye to my friend *Lazy*
  Time to grow myself some *Guts*.

© 2014

YOUR NEXT EXCUSE

There's something in there rattling
There's something in there loose
There's something in there tattling
  On your next excuse.

© 2014

PLURAL OF SPOUSE

If the plural of mouse is *mice*
And the plural of louse is *lice*
Is the plural of spouse then *spice*?

© 2015

Figure 23 - spice

CHASING STORMS

I was busy chasing storms
But much too close to see
As I was busy chasing storms
That storm I chased was me.

© 2015

Figure 24 - supercell rotations

A SPOT TO PRAY

For when my prayers are not enough
For when the soft in life turns tough
For when the smooth converts to rough

Find yourself a spot to pray
  Then pray and pray and pray and pray
    For your own deliverance.

© 2015

Figure 25 - Prayer

WHEN WILL I LEARN?

Grass so high it needs haying
Leaves so dry they could burn
For sloth and indolence I am paying
When, oh when, will I learn?

© 2015

Figure 26 - Mowers on the down-low

IS IT THAT

Is it that I'm mad,
..*Angry*
That makes me stay away.

Is it that I'm mad,
..*Crazy*
That I stay this way.

Is it that I'm sad,
..*Sorrowful*
At all that was so wrong.

Or is it that I'm bad,
..*Morally*
That I've stayed away so long?

© 2015

XANADU

Can I do
In Xanadu
What I cannot do elsewhere?

Figure 27 - Xanadu

AS YOU ARE NOW

I have loved
  As you are now
    Deeply lost in each other.

I have tossed
  The whole world over
    Hoping for another.

© 2015

Figure 28 - Love

MY ARDENT PLEA

I hereby send
  my ardent plea
    to those in Upper Room.

  I ask who's there
 to promptly free
Those caught in Satan's Gloom.

© 2015

Figure 29 - DRUNKEN

LIKE A FLAME

Perhaps it was
  You thought of me?
    I know I thought of you.

How like a flame
  Your love warms me
    Through and through and through.

© 2015

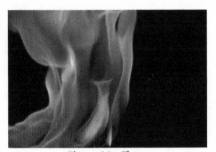

Figure 30 - Flame

NOTHING MUCH

There's nothing to my everything
Nothing much to see
But I have needed nothing much
(And it has needed me.)

© 2015

COOKIES

If they were good for you, *nutritious*
Not merely fattening, *delicious*
We wouldn't call them *cookies*.

© 2015

Figure 31 - Oatmeal cookies

THOSE THINGS
THAT MATTER

When your dreams all scatter
That's when you are shown
Those things that matter
(And those that don't.)

© 2015

LIKE THE COUNTRY MUSIC SINGER SAY

Just like the country music singer say
Wishing he could fall in love today
But he say you just get right in the way
(Just like the country music singer say.)

© 2015

Figure 32 - Hank Snow Statue

LISTEN TO THE BABBLING BROOK

Listen to the babbling brook
  He winds a weary tale
Note the plot, the theme, the hook
  The tone of distant dale.

Hear the lesson of the brook
  As you lose the plot
He carries bark from trees well shook
  (Items best forgot.)

© 2016

Figure 33 - Flowing Stream

HOW LIFE'S A COUNTRY SONG

Should I go a-wandering
To fix a life gone wrong
Or go on long a-pondering
How Life's a country song?

© 2016

Figure 34 - Country Music Television

WHICH WAY TO GO

I must have lived
. . here before
Though it was lives ago.

I know the dust,
. . the house, the road
I know which way to go.

© 2016

Figure 35 - Windsor, Vermont

REALLY ME?

Is this really me
Or is it me
Covering up the me
I don't want you to see?

© 2016

Figure 36 - Wooden mask

AS I CLEAVE YOU
TO MY BREAST

As I cleave you to my breast
As we filter out the rest
Can you see that this is best?
Can you see that we are blest?

© 2016

THINGS BEST
FORGOTTEN

Ever forgotten
.. where you were
Back from a dream
.. with things ablur
Remembering things
.. best forgotten?

© 2016

NIGHTTIME

Nighttime is for resting, sleeping
.. *Daily chore.*

Nighttime is for planning, scheming
.. *Walk the floor.*

Nighttime is for holding, hugging,
.. *Maybe more.*

Nighttime is for listening, fretting
.. *(Lock the door).*

© 2016

Figure 37 - Emptied

WHAT'S LEFT

What's left..
  When the shine is gone.

Bereft..
  Rusting on lawn.

No heft..
  Weak and drawn.

Once deft..
  Lost its brawn.

© 2016

Figure 38 - Jaguar

HEED THE WARNING

Birds fly south this morning
Triggered by the snow
Should I heed the warning
Or leave before I know?

© 2016

Figure 39 - flying geese

FEELING CHRISTMAS

Already feeling Christmas
Already seeing white
Already having Christmas thoughts
Cast their wondrous light.

© 2016

Figure 40 - Village at Mammoth

WHEN THE STORY'S WRITTEN

When the story's written
When the story's told
Tell 'em I was smitten
Tell 'em I was bold(!)

© 2016

Figure 41 - God Speed!

LET THE BLUEBIRDS IN

Leave the window open
Let the bluebirds in
When your dreams are broken
That's your chance to win.

© 2017

Figure 42 - Male western bluebird

IMAGES

Authors (rights)

38. jason goulding (CC BY 2.0)
39. liz west (CC BY 2.0)
40. Nandaro (CC BY-SA 3.0)
41. Edmund Leighton (1853–1922) (PD 80+)
42. Blalonde (CC BY-SA 4.0)

PD = Public Domain
CC = Creative Commons

ACKNOWLEDGEMENT

The author wishes to acknowledge all those who made this collection of verse possible — whether as impetus, critic, or appreciator.

ABOUT THE AUTHOR

Michael J. Farrand

In addition to poetic musings on life and love, the author turns his pen to prose, drama, and commentary.

His latest writings can be found at his blog, "Far an Few Between" at fewbetween.blog-spot.com

PRAISE FOR AUTHOR

"I have 'kissed' the love poems; so fine, delicate, but with a deep well beneath the words."

-JAMES FRASE-WHITE

"Lots of fun poems, a potpourri, some flip, some profound, and some about the heartbreak of lost love. Occasionally there's some stretching for rhyme, but it's all in good fun."

- S. J. CAHILL

"Funny!.. sweet.. strong & crisp.. pithy.. good.. cute.. clever!.. yes!.. witty.. excellent.. positive.. ends on a hopeful note"

- DONNA OTTO

"I was just taking a few minutes to concede a stalemate with the myriad tasks I'm plucking away at today, and decided to spend it leafing through this little book I had laying around entitled Until We Learn to Rise. I've got to say, 'A Country Lane' and 'Things Best Forgotten' are pretty good, and dare I say — worth the effort."

- TREVOR ROBINSON

"So, there I was, a couple of nights ago, lying in bed. I figured I'd read five or six of Mike's 60 short ditties before I turned off the light. But I couldn't put the book down! I had to read the whole book. It's what I've always thought poetry SHOULD be — something people can understand without driving themselves nuts trying to figure it out. Several of the poems made me laugh right out loud. Each one is deft. Each one is fun. In a nutshell, the book is terrific."

- JERRY JOHNSON

"Got your book for my birthday, perfection." + "Got your book fresh off the press, and I read it in one sitting.."

- SIMON HARRISON

"Until We Learn to Rise landed this morning, and I'm reading it almost as I write to thank you! I admire your wit and vulnerability, the surprises poem to poem."

- GEOF HEWITT

POETRY BOOKS

Verse on life, love, philosophy, and art in diverse lengths and forms.

The Man Who Didn't Exist

Sixty or so quatrains by Michael J. Farrand on a variety of topics, e.g., love, life, place, wheels, and philosophy. Some are light, some are a bit deeper. All are quick. Each poem is paired with an image to add perspective and interest.

Until We Learn To Rise

Short poems by Michael J. Farrand on life and love.

Greatest Unsolved Mystery

Variety of poems by Michael J. Farrand on life, love, etc. — many with carefully-selected images.

Hope Springs Eternal Still

A collection of beat, sentence, and word poems by Michael J. Farrand.

Made in the USA
Middletown, DE
03 May 2021

38036380R00047